IMAGES OF ENGLAND

NUNEATON
REVISITED

Under an order of the Court of Chancery

Made in the Causes Walker v. Aston, Aston v. Hazlehurst, and Aston v. Walker,

IN EIGHT LOTS.

Particulars and Conditions of Sale

OF

The Nuneaton & Attleborough Estate,

IN THE

COUNTY OF WARWICK,

EIGHT MILES FROM COVENTRY, TWO OF HINCKLEY, AND IMMEDIATELY ADJOINING

THE FAMOUS MANUFACTURING

TOWN OF NUNEATON,

IT COMPREHENDS

Four superior FARMS,

EXTENDING TO

1205 Acres of excellent Land,

(GREAT PART EXEMPT FROM TITHE),

And the whole of a convertible Soil, with Residences and Buildings of a first-rate character, and a Tenantry quite unexceptionable ; also the moiety of the

Manors of Nuneaton and Attleborough,

AND THE

STONE QUARRY,

With the Royalties connected therewith ; and the

VALUABLE MINERALS.

The present inadequate net Receipt of the whole Estate is upwards of

£2350 A YEAR,

And is one of the most eligible, compact, and profitable Estates in the Market, and a capital exchange for

THREE PER CENTS. AT PAR;

It will be Sold by Auction, by

Mr. GEO. ROBINS,

At the AUCTION MART, opposite the Bank of England,

On TUESDAY, the 30th day of JULY, 1844,

By direction of SIR WILLIAM HORNE, one of the Masters of the High Court of Chancery,

AT TWELVE O'CLOCK, IN EIGHT LOTS.

Particulars, with Plans and Conditions of Sale, to be had at the said Master's Office, in Southampton Buildings, Chancery Lane, London ; of Messrs. SMITH and ATKINS, 12, Sergeant's Inn, London ; Messrs. HODDING, HODDING and TOWNSEND, Salisbury ; Messrs. KEEN and HAND, Stafford ; Messrs. WHITE, EYRE and WHITE, Bedford Row, London ; Messrs. SLATER and HEELIS, Manchester ; Mr. RADFORD, Solicitor, Atherstone ; the Craven Arms, Coventry ; Spread Eagle, Rugby ; the Midland Counties' Herald and General Advertiser Office, Birmingham ; of Mr. R. STELFOX, Surveyor, Allesley ; the Auction Mart, and at MR. GEO. ROBINS' Offices, Covent Garden, London.

(ALFRED ROBINS, PRINTER, 101, LONG ACRE.)

IMAGES OF ENGLAND

NUNEATON
REVISITED

PETER LEE

TEMPUS

First published 2006

Tempus Publishing Limited
The Mill, Brimscombe Port,
Stroud, Gloucestershire, GL5 2QG
www.tempus-publishing.com

British Library Cataloguing in Publication Data.
A catalogue record for this book is available from the British Library.

ISBN 0 7524 3979 0

Typesetting and origination by Tempus Publishing Limited.
Printed in Great Britain.

Contents

Acknowledgements

I would like to thank all those who have provided photographs from their collections: the late Geoff Edmands, Ronald Edmands, Peter Bayly, Phillip Vernon, Reg Rowley, Maurice Billington, Reg Bull, Mick Lee, Fred Phillips, and Alan Croshaw. For the continuous generous help of my friend – Alan Cook. Also to Madge Edmands, Rod Grubb, Anne Paling Lawson, Pat Roberts, John Burton, Steve Casey, and Keith Draper for their contribution, both for supplying photographs and information. To Tony Parratt at the *Heartland Evening News*, and the staff of the *Coventry Evening Telegraph*. Also thanks to the knowledgeable staff of Nuneaton Library where I have carried out most of my local research.

Introduction

In 2007 Nuneaton celebrates three important anniversaries.

The famous Chilvers Coton authoress, George Eliot (1819–1880), made her first venture into popular print 150 years ago. *Scenes of Clerical Life* was serialised in *Blackwood's Magazine* in 1857.

The 100th anniversary of the Incorporation of Nuneaton as a borough takes place in 2007. Along with this there will also be celebrations of the opening in 1907 of Riversley Park.

Another selection of views of our local district will celebrate these anniversaries, and will, I hope, entertain you, your family, and old Nuneatonians spread far and wide.

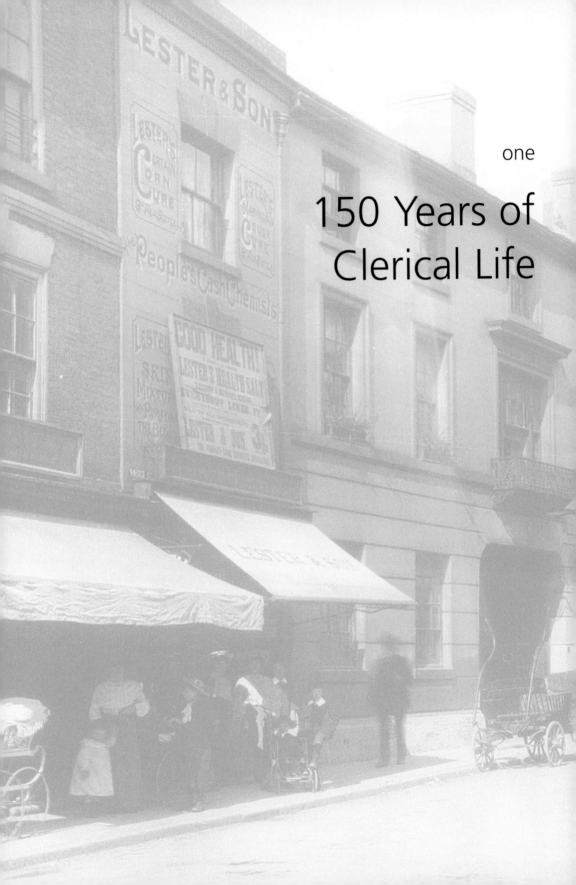

one

150 Years of
Clerical Life

'The Real Drama of Evangelicalism – and it has abundance of fine Drama for any one who has genius enough to discern and reproduce it – lies among the middle and lower classes', wrote Mary Ann Evans (1819-1880) who went on to become George Eliot, one of the finest novelists of the Victorian age. Her first series of stories later gathered together in a three-part book *Scenes of Clerical Life* centered on parish life in three Nuneaton parishes – Chilvers Coton, Astley and Nuneaton. The middle and lower classes referred to were those in her home district she now painted into those *Scenes of Clerical Life* which was first serialised in *Blackwood's Magazine* from January to November 1857. At first only a single copy of *Blackwood's Magazine* was circulating in Nuneaton but the recipient of this literary magazine soon noticed allusions to local life and events which seemed to have been written by someone who still lived in the district. For Miss Evans writing under the *nom de plume* 'George Eliot', remote from her native town and district, in London, who felt safe from any brickbats which this series of stories might bring, was shocked to find an unprecedented storm of trouble brewing up which was as dramatic as anything she might have expected to write about in any future novel. The literary people of Nuneaton went looking for the author. Struggling to find anyone who could have written it they foisted their attention on Joseph Liggins. Joe was probably unique in Nuneaton at that time as having gone to Cambridge, had rusticated, and was now living alone in Attleborough supposedly engaged in writing a book. Surprised by the attention he was now receiving and feeling that claiming the authorship might only find him good entry to the best company and largesse in his home district, he foolishly concurred that he was the author. The whole thing got out of hand. Letters were written to Blackwood's complaining that their poor storyteller had not received a penny in royalties from his work. Various local dignitaries including the Revd James Quirk, the vicar of Attleborough, and Charles Holte Bracebridge of Atherstone, a foolish and noisy aristocrat, wrote letters to *The Times*. In the end Miss Evans had to admit the authorship to put paid to all this nonsense, and that was that. Joe Liggins slipped back into poverty and the people of Nuneaton, Chilvers Coton and Astley back into obscurity.

After George Eliot died in 1880 more and more people started to tour the district looking for local landmarks associated with the stories she had written. In 1888 one such researcher, S. Parkinson, wrote a book, *Scenes from the George Eliot Country* where he wrote:

'Nuneaton is neither ignorant of, nor indifferent to, the distinction that has come to it by reason of George Eliot's associations with the district … but while you would search the town in vain for a scrap of printed matter, the chances are that the first adult person you met in the street would give you much of the information you required.

Having spent three days visiting the town in the 1880s he came across a local who said, 'Oh, yes … all the people in *Scenes of Clerical Life* are real. Dead and gone now, but with relatives still living in the town'.

MARKET PLACE.

The Market Place has been the hub of local life for 900 years and is still today the focus of attention for visitors to the area. When Clare Speight took this photograph it was very similar to George Eliot's memory of it. The most noticeable feature on the right is the former Market House, with its bell tower and weather vane, the predecessor of the town hall. Built by public subscription in 1819 it would have been very much as Miss Evans remembered it from her school days at Miss Wallington's School in Church Street between the years 1828-1832. A tour around this picture starts on the left with the White Swan, one of the eleven pubs in or around the Market Place; there are three immediately noticeable in this view. Beyond that is Messrs Mason Bros, the drapers. The three-storey building set back slightly with the stuccoed front was Smith's Charity School (the headmaster at this time was Thomas Daffern). It was still functioning at this date having been founded by Richard Smith, a native of Nuneaton, by a bequest in his will of 1716 to educate the poor children of Nuneaton. Beyond that the taller building was Craddock & Bull's Bank (at this date the Birmingham & Midland Counties Banking Co.) which was the predecessor of today's Barclays Bank. The light coloured two-storey building in the far distance is the Crystal Palace public house. In Miss Evans' memory it would have been the Hare & Squirrel. In the eighteenth century it was called the Plough. Hidden from view on the left-hand side there were three public houses. The Old Ram dated back to the time of the Abbey and closed in the 1870s. The White Hart, another very old pub, was a scene of radicalism amongst the working classes of Nuneaton and associated with the poor unfortunate Mary Ball who was publicly hung at Coventry in 1849 for administering poison to her abusive husband. Her story can also be traced as a character in George Eliot's *Adam Bede* published in 1858. Mary was the last woman to be publicly hung in Warwickshire. It is remarkable to think that from her one surviving child there is a large group of her descendents alive today. The Castle was more of an inn than a pub, which opened in 1832 and closed in 1963. It provided accommodation but probably to commercial travellers rather than the upper classes and gentry who stayed at the two commercial hotels in town – the Newdigate and the Bull.

It is strange to remember that the three pubs stood next door to one another. Just beyond the Crystal Palace in what was then Queen's Street (now Queen's Road) was the Red Lion. A collection of shops to the right of the Crystal Palace were the Fish Supply Stores, J. Jones, grocer & provision dealer, and a well-known firm Shute & Sons, clothiers.

In between these shops and descending down the left-hand side of buildings to the Market House stood three more pubs. The Grapes and the Board were merged although the Board was demolished in 1956. Next to the Board the low gable ends of the Peacock can just be seen. This very old pub was used as a staging post for at least one firm of carriers to and from Coventry in the nineteenth century before the railway killed the horse-drawn carriage trade. It was rebuilt in the 1930s as a modern pub. The shop before you get to the Market House was in the occupation of Ezekiel Haddon, grocer & wine merchant. It was at the Market House that the market's affairs were administered and it had a commodious function room for local dances and events, political meetings and light entertainment. It is hard to imagine that it, too, had its own public house – the Market House Inn – although it hardly seems credible that a town this size justified it. The buildings to the right of the Market House would have been renewed after Miss Evans' time in the 1840s. Prior to that the 1840s block of buildings in this section of the Market Place contained another pub, the Plough, which was surrounded by the fixed butchers' shambles. These were permanent stalls where the butchers vended their meats on market days. Animals driven into the Market Place were killed in the street in full view of the public so the meat was still very fresh and warm when cut up and sold to the market-goers.

The road going off to the right, now Newdigate Square, was once called Pie Corner from its associations with the ancient Court of Piepoudre where, in medieval times, the administration of the fair and market was carried out. Incidentally the bell on the Market House was a necessary concomitant of municipal life in those days. Its meager tinkling brought residents to the market on certain days of the year for ceremonial occasions, or rarely if there was a national disaster such as the sovereign dying, being crowned or married. It was also used to summon aid if a fire had broken out or some other kind of disaster had occurred. Later on its tinkling was described as 'paltry' and there was great relief when it was removed to make way for the smart new building and clock seen today. The money from the sale of the Market House was put into a fund which sat in the bank for thirty years until a new municipal building was built in 1932 in Coton Road – the council house, now the town hall. On the right is A & A Smith the grocer & tobacconist (demolished in 1909) and on the right just visible is William Cawthorne, printer & stationer. Cawthorne's business originated in the 1830s with Thomas Short on whose death he was superseded by his wife Mary who sold it to Edward Houlston. In the 1860s it was taken over by William Cawthorne. The business is still trading and is one of Nuneaton's oldest surviving family businesses. (Clare Speight)

The Market Place, 1910, looking towards Bridge Street showing the town's distinctive clock on the left. On the extreme left are the low gables of the Peacock. Through the archway under the clock is Boffin's Arcade where once stood the Market House Inn, later known as the Clock.

Beyond that on the corner leading to what is now Newdigate Square was the old Plough Inn. When it closed its name was transferred to the Golden Ball in Abbey Street. It had a large framework sign with a gilded ball hanging from it to which was added a plough. The pub then became known as the Plough and Ball. (Its lineal descendent today is the Town Talk). Stretching up Bridge Street is the Bull Inn and on the right-hand side were the White Swan, demolished in the 1960s and the Ram, demolished in the 1870s. Other pubs along Bridge Street were the White Hart and the Castle. Behind the camera was the Crystal Palace, previously known as the Hare & Squirrel until it was jazzed up to became a music hall. Behind the camera and a few yards up Queen's Road was the Red Lion and out of view just a few yards up Coventry Street was the original Nags Head. (Author's collection)

A view of Bridge Street from the Market Place before 1900. Yoxall's cake and pie shop was on the left and next to it Lester & Sons, chemists & druggists, who later moved across the Market Place to where the Marks & Spencer store is today. On the opposite corner is the old post office which was demolished in 1912 when a larger post office was built nearby. It is appropriate that the post office should be located so close to the Bull as before the post office was opened mail business was conducted from the Bull. The Bull continued as a parcels office for the London & North Western Railway into the 1900s. (Author's collection)

CAWTHORNE'S FAMILY ALMANACK, 1889.

4, BRIDGE ST., NUNEATON.

WILLIAM WHEATLEY,

BOOT & SHOE MAKER

AND

LEATHER SELLER.

BESPOKE

ORDERS AND REPAIRS

PROMPTLY ATTENDED TO.

Opposite: The Bull Inn doorway. It was here that many stage coaches drew up in the nineteenth century so that their passengers could enjoy a meal or an overnight stay. (Claire Speight)

THE "RED LION" of GEORGE ELIOT.

in the bar of which Lawyer Dempster and his
friends were wont to meet. From the large
upper window "the public-spirited attorney"
harangued the crowd whom he incited to
violently oppose the Sunday-evening lectures
at Milby Church, and called for "three cheers
for True Religion and down with cant".
"I am a man of deeds' (ay, dam you, that
you are, and you charge well for 'em too,"
said a voice from the crowd, probably
that of a gentleman who was immediately
afterwards observed with his hat crushed
over his head.)

                              Janet's Repentance.
                                  (Chap 4).

THE CHURCH AND VICARAGE, NUNEATON.

St Nicolas parish church. Within the last fifty years the 'h' in Nicholas has disappeared from common use. It was the parish church in Milby, being the traditional church where the good people of that parish worshipped and wherein Miss Evans observed in *Janet's Repentance*, 'the standard of morality at Milby, you perceive, was not inconveniently high in those good old times, and an ingenuous vice or two was what every man expected of his neighbour'. The church remains today a key feature of the town. The silent sleepers in the graveyard could bear testimony if their spirits could speak of the reality behind Miss Evans' stories.

Opposite above: Nuneaton Vicarage around 1890. George Eliot's characters, Mr and Mrs Crewe, were in reality the curate of Nuneaton, the Revd Hugh Hughes (1779-1830), and his wife. Revd Hughes was also headmaster at the adjacent grammar school. Here upon the lawn is gathered the family of Revd Henry Bellairs. The Revd Bellaire's father, vicar of Bedworth, appeared in *Scenes* as Mr Fellowes. (Author's collection)

Right: Revd Henry Walford Bellairs, (1812-1900) was appointed vicar of Nuneaton in 1872 and served the community for twenty-one years until his retirement in 1893. With quill in hand he looks as though he is about to commence writing a lengthy sermon. He was born in Twickenham but the family anciently came from Kirby Bellairs in Leicestershire. He married Mary Hannah Albina Kenrick and had at least four children – Kenneth Farrington, Constance, Hylda and Maud. After he left Nuneaton he became Canon of Worcester Cathedral. During his stay at Nuneaton he wrote a booklet in verse, *Traditions of Nuneaton and Its Neighbourhood*, published by Frederick Duncan Robertson who was proprietor of the *Nuneaton Chronicle*.

Above: Between 1828 and 1832 Church Street (or Orchard Street in *Scenes*) was the centre of Miss Evans' life. It was in Orchard Street where some of the best people lived and the place where much of the intrigue centered upon *Janet's Repentance*. This view from around 1880 shows the Marquis of Granby pub newly rebuilt on the right, but elsewhere the buildings go back to Miss Evans' time. The frontage with the prominent gable was erected in 1860. It was the lawyer's office of John Estlin, a prominent townsman who supplanted the later business of the infamous 'Lawyer Dempster'.

At the rear of Mr Pettifer's house was this verandah under which 'Janet' sheltered after being turned out by her husband 'Lawyer Dempster'. These premises were demolished after the great Nuneaton Blitz in 1941. (Author's collection)

Opposite below: Looking in the opposite direction towards the town centre in May 1959, a scene that would shortly be swept away except for the Queen's Head pub on the left, later the Pen & Wig, and the buildings in the far distance which are now the Nationwide Building Society. In the 1950s this road was the main thoroughfare through Nuneaton giving access to Leicester Road from Attleborough Road. There was no ring road and Vicarage Street was still a narrow back road. The buildings on the right including the Kings Head pub were demolished in 1960. The light coloured building in the middle distance on the left-hand side was the Marquis of Granby more commonly known as the Granby. Beyond this is the narrow defile of Bridge Street leading to the Market Place. No yellow lines were needed because cars did not impinge that much on the road system to need restrictions, and street parking was available in most parts of town. On the vacant lot in the left of the picture can be seen the gable end of a house which was badly damaged in the Blitz and demolished just after the Second World War. This was the residence of John Robinson who was Mr Pettifer in *Scenes*. (Reg Bull, *Coventry Evening Telegraph*)

Above and opposite: The familiar front door of Lawyer Dempster's House. George Eliot stated 'His house lay in Orchard Street which opened on the prettiest outskirts of town – the church, the parsonage, and a long stretch of green fields'. At the outbreak of the Second World War it was owned by Mr F.N. Iliffe who gave it its name, Lawyer Dempster's House. In 1941 it was very badly damaged by bombing and was subsequently demolished. Had it not been, I feel sure it would have provided a fine reminder of the old town so much associated with our great author.

Lawyer Dempster in real life was the blend of two local townsmen who really existed. The name comes from Dempster Heming, a character who figured large in the life of the town in the 1820s and 1830s. He was the Registrar of Calcutta who, with great wealth made in the sub-continent, returned to his native district and purchased a modest estate at Caldecote just north east of Nuneaton fronting Watling Street. He featured in George Eliot's *Felix Holt, the Radical* published in 1866 and later Harold Transome was modelled on him.

But in *Scenes of Clerical Life* the Dempster character is less redeeming. The original was also a lawyer James Williams Buchanan (1792-1846), as apparently Miss Evans later wrote, 'Dempster is too barefaced a brute and I am sorry that the poor wife's sufferings should have driven her to so unsentimental a resource as beer'. It was at the bar of the Red Lion where Lawyer Dempster consumed great quantities of brandy. It would be interesting to know how Miss Evans' pen picture of Mr Dempster closely resembled that of James W. Buchanan, the real-life character she based this personage upon:

> He was a tall and very massive man, and the front half of his large surface was so well drudged with snuff, that the cat, having inadvertently come near him, had then been seized with a severe fit of sneezing … Mr Dempster habitually held his chin tucked in, and his head hanging forward, weighed down, perhaps by a preponderant occiput and a bulging forehead, between which his closely clipped coronal surface lay like a flat and new mown table land.

Her model for 'Janet' was Mrs Buchanan. (Clare Speight)

LAWYER DEMPSTERS HOUSE

NUNEATON.

(SCENES OF CLERICAL LIFE
"JANETS REPENTANCE")
CHAPS 14 & 15

WHEN THRUST OUT BY ————— ····
DEMPSTER INTO "THE STONY
STREET", THE BITTER NORTH -
EAST WIND AND DARKNESS·
THE HARSH WIND CUTTING
HER NAKED FEET AND DRIVING HER LONG HAIR
AWAY FROM HER HALF-CLAD BOSOM - - - JANET
SAT SHIVERING ON THE DOORSTONE, WITH THE DOOR SHUT
UPON HER PAST LIFE, AND THE FUTURE BLACK AND UNSHAPEN ————

NUNEATON · CHILVERS COTON
PARISH CHURCH.

Above: Milly's Grave. Milly Barton was the wife of Amos Barton, the vicar at Shepperton. She died and left six poor children as did the real Milly – Mrs Emma Gwyther wife of the real vicar Revd John Gwyther. George Eliot wrote of her, 'The flowing lines of her tall slender figure made the limpest dress look graceful, and her old frayed black silk seemed to repose on her bust and limbs with placid elegance and sense of distinction'. Emma died on 4 November 1836 aged thirty-four. George Eliot prepared a tender reverence as Mr Gwyther (the Revd Amos Barton), returned to the grave and said, 'Milly, Milly dost thou hear me? I didn't love thee enough, I wasn't tender enough to thee, but I think of it all now'. The grave can still be seen in Chilvers Coton churchyard and has been repaired in recent years. (Clare Speight)

Opposite above: Shepperton church (Chilvers Coton). The parish church of All Saints, Chilvers Coton, was a fine old country church. The original apart from the distinctive clock tower has been lost. Incendiary bombs destroyed the old church of Miss Evans' day on the night of 16/17 May 1941 by the Luftwaffe in a large raid on Nuneaton. One old-timer in Nuneaton recalled to me his memories of that night. He sought shelter as best he could, as the bombs came down under Coton Arches railway bridge. He said the incendiary bombs clattered on to the church roof and took a long time to take hold. If he had had a ladder he could have climbed on the roof and flung them off. But where was he to find a ladder in the middle of an air raid? That is if he had the recklessness to scurry about looking for one, with incendiaries and high explosive bombs falling all around the town.

The church was rebuilt after the war, but not to the original pattern, which was a great pity. There are several parts of the churchyard which are reminders of old Chilvers Coton. It is a country churchyard still, despite now being hemmed in by houses and factories. (Author's collection)

Opposite below: Reg Bull and Geoff Edmands – two prominent local photographers whose work has featured in local books a great deal lately. The photograph taken on 5 June 1955 at South Farm, Arbury, George Eliot's birthplace. (Geoff Edmands)

Robert Evans' Grave. Mary Ann Evans' father was Robert Evans (1773-1849) who was estate agent to the Newdigate family and various local landowners. He came to Chilvers Coton from Derbyshire after the Newdigate estate had been inherited by a nephew of the late Sir Roger Newdigate who died childless in 1806. In 1809 his wife, Harriett Poynton, died in childbirth with their third child who also died shortly thereafter. In 1813 Robert Evans remarried his second wife Christiana Pearson, the youngest daughter of Isaac Pearson, a yeoman of Astley. He had five more children including Mary Ann Evans, but two boys lived only ten days. After Robert Evans retired and passed the business to his son Isaac, he went to live in Coventry, but his body was interred in Chilvers Coton.

Opposite above: Arbury Hall – home of the Newdigates. The Newdigate family originally acquired the estate in 1586. Sir Roger Newdigate (1719-1806) encased the original Elizabethan house within a Gothicised façade, spending a fortune on it. Work started in 1748 and was completed just before his death in 1805. Sir Roger's parliamentary career lasted thirty-five years. George Eliot transformed Arbury into Cheveral Manor in *Scenes of Clerical Life*. The Newdigates became the Oldinport family.

Opposite below: Dorlcote Mill at Arbury was the original for the *Mill on the Floss* from which George Eliot Drew from her childhood memories, 'with its great heaps of corn for little girls to slide upon and its family of fat, flour dusted spiders'. (Author's collection)

ARBURY HALL, NUNEATON

Arbury Mill, "George Eliots Writings"   Nuneaton

Above: The church on Paddiford Common. (Stockingford chapel of ease). To the west of Nuneaton town there was a large expanse of poor heathland, a moonscape of clay holes, shallow coal pits, scrubby hedgerows, tumbledown farms and scatterings of poor cottages. This outlying district stretched over to Arbury woods and out across towards the villages of Ansley and Hartshill. The edges of this area were ill-defined but all came under the general title – Nuneaton Common – broken down into smaller parts such as Heath End, Stockingford Common and Galley Common. The latter is well known today and still retains a reminder of the old common land. By the 1800s the population of Stockingford was starting to expand. The hamlet itself was a straggling quantity of cottages perhaps more closely spaced along what is now Church Road descending to the Lamb & Flag public house, but towards Nuneaton along Swan Lane (Croft Road) and the 'old lane' now Haunchwood Road, the houses were sparse. The one-mile walk on a Sunday must have been a deterrent to all but the hardiest travellers in Nuneaton to go to church so it was decided that religion should be taken to the people of Stockingford. A chapel of ease was built and opened in 1824. In 1843 Stockingford became an ecclesiastical parish in its own right. The curate attached to the new church was John Edmund Jones (1797-1831) whose oratory was livelier and more interesting than that delivered by the perpetual curate at Nuneaton church. The congregation at the mother church made the tracks to Stockingford to hear Mr Jones. It was a great conversation piece at the time and George Eliot records it in *Janet's Repentance*. (Author's Collection)

Opposite above and below: Griff House. When Robert Evans came to Griff in 1806 his first home was at South Farm, Arbury where his daughter Mary Ann Evans was born in 1819. In 1820 the Evans family moved to a larger home, Griff House, which stood on the high road between Bedworth and Nuneaton. At that time Griff was a quite rural backwater where the twitter of birds and buzz of wildlife were only interrupted by the clank of steam engines from the nearby Griff coal pits and the rumble of horses and carts. Elegant stage coaches passed by on the turnpike road to Coventry. Griff House itself has now been converted into a hotel but it is a remarkable survivor with the ancient farmhouse still standing at the rear together with the original dairy and various outbuildings associated with the farm. When S. Parkinson visited in 1888, Isaac Evans was still alive and the property was still as his sister would have remembered it as a child:

Nearby the brown canal where
Slowly the barges floated into view,
Rounding a grassy hill to me sublime,
With some unknown beyond it, whither flew
The parting cuckoo toward a fresh spring time.

Above: The brown canal which George Eliot remembered as a working canal was probably the Griff Arm of the Coventry Canal. Here the Swan and Bunting narrow boats negotiate the tight bridge at Griff Hollows along the Griff Arm as they float empty of coal on 21 February 1960. (Geoff Edmands)

Right: Another part of old Coton was the lane now known as Avenue Road but then called Coton Lane lying on the Attleborough side of the Wem Brook and Church Lane on the Coton side. (It ran beside Coton Church.) In 1900 it was a quiet leafy lane with high banks either side, and I recall these high banks were still extant on the Coton side in the 1960s until the road was widened and the sidewalks greatly altered. (Author's collection)

Below: A little later the whole road was called Avenue Road and here the road crossed the Wem Brook by a narrow bridge. This was arranged so that horses could go down to the brook for a drink and you can see this happening on the right-hand side of the bridge. The date would be around 1910. (Author's collection)

Opposite below: The Lady Bridge on the Griff Arm on 9 January 1959. (Geoff Edmands)

Coton Lane, Nuneaton.

AVENUE ROAD,
Attleborough, Near Nuneaton.

Griff Hollows was the stretch of Coventry Road from the bottom of the hill going out of Coton to the hamlet of Griff where it crossed the Griff Arm of the Coventry Canal. The bridge is behind the photographer. This view shows one of Coton's old pubs, the Newdigate Inn, or more colloquially The Bloody Hand after the Newdigate family's heraldic shield which it displayed on its signboard. This was a red Fleur de Lys which had the appearance of a red clawed hand to our ancestors as they viewed it from a distance.

When this photograph was taken around 1905 it was no longer a pub. Its license seems to have been abandoned about 1860. (Author's collection)

The traditions of Chilvers Coton were made in its old pubs and public buildings. A great deal of interest centered on the Wharf Inn, which was built at the time of the Coventry Canal. This view was photographed after 1925 when the canal bridge was widened but before the 1930s when the block just visible on the right was knocked down. It had formerly been used as a barrack block for boatmen where they could get a good night's sleep on *terra firma* after weeks spent afloat. It was here after a night or day on Eadies Burton Ales (it later became a Bass pub) that they could retreat to their straw palisades in the barracks block and sleep it off. There was also a boat repair facility and warerooms where goods could be stored after delivery from the canal or before being dispatched that way. (Author's collection)

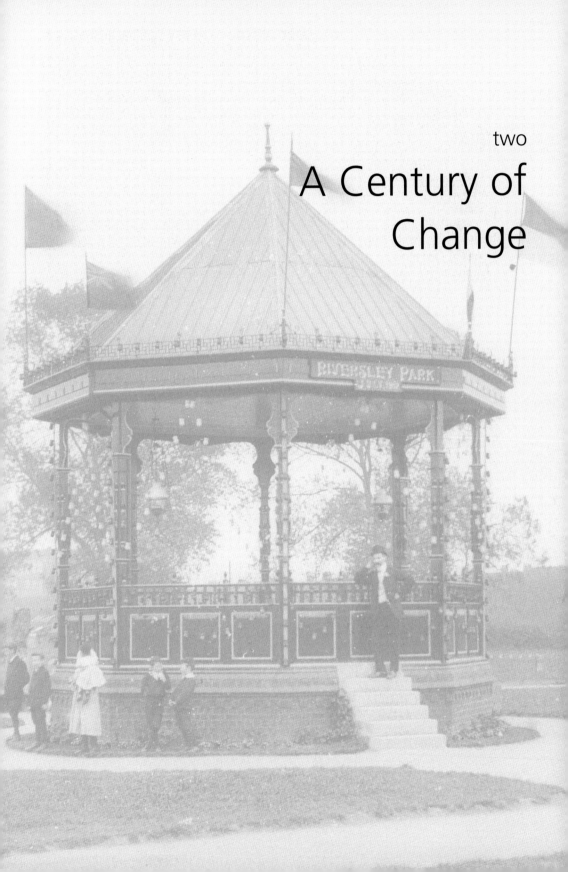

two

A Century of Change

In 2007 Nuneaton celebrates the centenary of its formation as a borough. It had previously been an Urban District Council. In 1974 the borough was enlarged by the inclusion of the adjacent mining town of Bedworth to form the modern borough. In 2006 the borough had a combined population of 119,000.

Work started on the town becoming a borough in 1901 and it took six years for the planning and implementation to be completed. King Edward VII granted the incorporation of charter status on 22 July 1907 following a petition presented by leading inhabitants and householders of the town. The new status was necessary because in twenty years the population had more than doubled from 11,469 in 1881 to 24,996 in 1901.

In 1907 the whole town was excited and embraced its new status with open arms. The sleepy backwater was rapidly becoming a modern metropolis. To celebrate its new status a large area of open ground through which the river Anker ran was given to the town and laid out as a new park by Alderman Edward Ferdinand Melly (1858-1941), the managing director of Griff Collieries. Riversley Park also celebrates its anniversary in 2007 having been opened to the public in July 1907.

The first meeting of the new borough council was held at noon on 9 November 1907.

CAWTHORNE'S FAMILY ALMANACK, 1890.

WINTER SEASON.

C. PARSONS,

WHOLESALE AND GENERAL

AGRICULTURAL AND

MANUFACTURING IRONMONGER,

NUNEATON,

Calls attention to his Stock of

HEATING STOVES

Suitable for Churches, Chapels, and Workshops;

ALSO TO HIS STOCK OF

CHAFF CUTTERS,	OIL CAKE MILLS,
TURNIP CUTTERS,	CORN GRINDING MILLS,
TURNIP PULPERS,	HORSE GEARS,

AND EVERY DESCRIPTION OF

AGRICULTURAL IMPLEMENTS.

Estimates given for Heating Buildings, Conservatories, &c.,
by Hot Water,

AND FOR ALL DESCRIPTIONS OF

IRON FENCING, HURDLES, PALISADING, &c.

AGENT FOR THE SALE OF

BLASTING POWDER, DYNAMITE, FUSE,

And Dealer in all kinds of

COLLIERY AND BRICKYARD REQUISITES.

Above: The old Market House before it
was sold in 1899 for £13,125.

CRWINUENE FAMILI ALMANAUA, 1071.

ESTABLISHED 1833.

T. ILIFFE AND SON,

PHARMACEUTICAL & DISPENSING

CHEMISTS,

MARKET-PLACE, NUNEATON.

Strict regard is paid to the Purity of the Drugs employed in Dispensing.

AGENTS FOR SCHWEPPE AND CO'S AND

All Kinds of FOREIGN MINERAL WATERS,

LEIBIG COMPANY'S

EXTRACT OF MEAT,

For the immediate production of excellent Beef Tea, of superior flavour, and cheaper than that prepared from fresh meat. This article was introduced into this Neighbourhood by us a few years ago, as one worthy of our recommendation, not only as being most useful for domestic purposes, but also on account of its immense value as a restorative agent during and after illness; sold in 2-oz. jars, 1/9, ¼-lb., 3/2, ½-lb. 6/0, 1-lb. 11/0. Leibig's Extract of Meat Biscuits, Leibig's Malted Food Extract, Leibig's, Du Barry's, Dr. Ridge's, and Hard's Food for Infants and Invalids; Chapman and Co's Entire Wheat Flour; Epps's Cocoa; Bragg's Prepared Vegetable Charcoal and Biscuits; The Anglo Swiss Company's Condensed Milk; Parrish's Compound Syrup of Phosphates or Chemical Food; Pepsine and Pepsine Wine; Lamplough's Pyretic Saline; Riggolot's Mustard Leaves, a convenient and efficient substitute for mustard poultices.

PATENT MEDICINES, Fancy Soaps & Perfumes

Foreign Eau de Cologne, (the Original and Best) English do. with a Patent Sprinkler attached,—French Essences for the Handkerchief, of various kinds and of the best quality, in original bottles as imported.—Piesse and Lubin's concentrated Essence of the Sacred Lign Aloe, and Opoponax, in bottles, 2/6 each.—The Mona Bouquet, &c.

BEST TOOTH, NAIL, HAIR, AND SHAVING BRUSHES. THE PANSTREPTON BATH BRUSH, AND DO. FOR NURSERY.

Turkey and Honey Comb Sponges, all sizes, and of finest quality.—Chest Protectors Sponge Bags, Washing Gloves, Oxford Washing Pads, Calefacio Belts, Dr. Nelson's Inhalers.—Elastic Stockings, Knee Caps, Ankle Pieces, Trusses, Enemas and Surgical appliances of every description—Prices on application. Silver mounted Smelling Bottles, Wickered Scent Bottles for the Pocket.—Glycerine Jelly, a new and elegant preparation for softening the skin, is pleasant to use, and an excellent preventive of chapped lips and hands, sold in pots at 6d. and 1/ each.—Glycerine and Lime Cream the favourite preparation for the Hair, combining the properties of Hair-Wash and Pomade.—Glycerine and Cantharidine Lotion for cleansing the skin of the head and promoting the growth of the Hair.—Quinine Dentifrice for cleaning and preserving the Teeth from decay, and all other Toilet requisites.

MANUFACTURERS OF THE ORANGE QUININE WINE.—This pleasant Tonic has won a high and deserved reputation which has secured for it an extensive and constantly increasing sale; Cod Liver Oil taken with this Wine sits more easily on the Stomach.—Finest New Cod Liver Oil, of very superior quality and nearly tasteless.—Qualitative and Quantitative Analysis of Well, Spring, River, or other Waters, for Drinking, Domestic, or Manufacturing purposes.—Test for presence of Arsenic in Paper-Hangings, also Analysis of Poisoned Animals, Poisoned Food, &c.

HORSE & CATTLE MEDICINES of every description. Any proprietary preparation of repute, not kept in stock, will be procured at request, as early as possible.

Above and opposite: The Market Place was enlivened with bunting, flags and all the trappings of a town fast becoming one of the most important in Warwickshire. The older businesses supplanted by new ones; W. & R. Fletchers, the butchers, The Maypole Dairy Co. Ltd, and the Grand Clothing Hall, the largest tailors in the kingdom, which sold everything for the gentleman of distinction. The structure in the centre of the picture fitted with white glazed bricks was a drinking fountain. The iron ladle on a chain used for drinking had acquired an unsanitary reputation and was known as the 'fever cup'. In 1940 the fountain was removed and the water supply used for an air-raid standpipe. The celebrations themselves took place on Saturday 28 September 1907.

The "Nuneaton Advertiser"

Published every SATURDAY Morning, and Sold by

WM. CAWTHORNE,

PRINTER AND BOOKSELLER, MARKET PLACE, NUNEATON.

PRICE ONE PENNY.

The LARGEST, CHEAPEST, & BEST FAMILY NEWSPAPER, in the Neighbourhood.

Circulating in the Towns of Nuneaton, Atherstone, Rugby, Tamworth, &c., &c.

AN EXCELLENT ADVERTISING MEDIUM.

ADVERTISEMENTS SOLICITED.

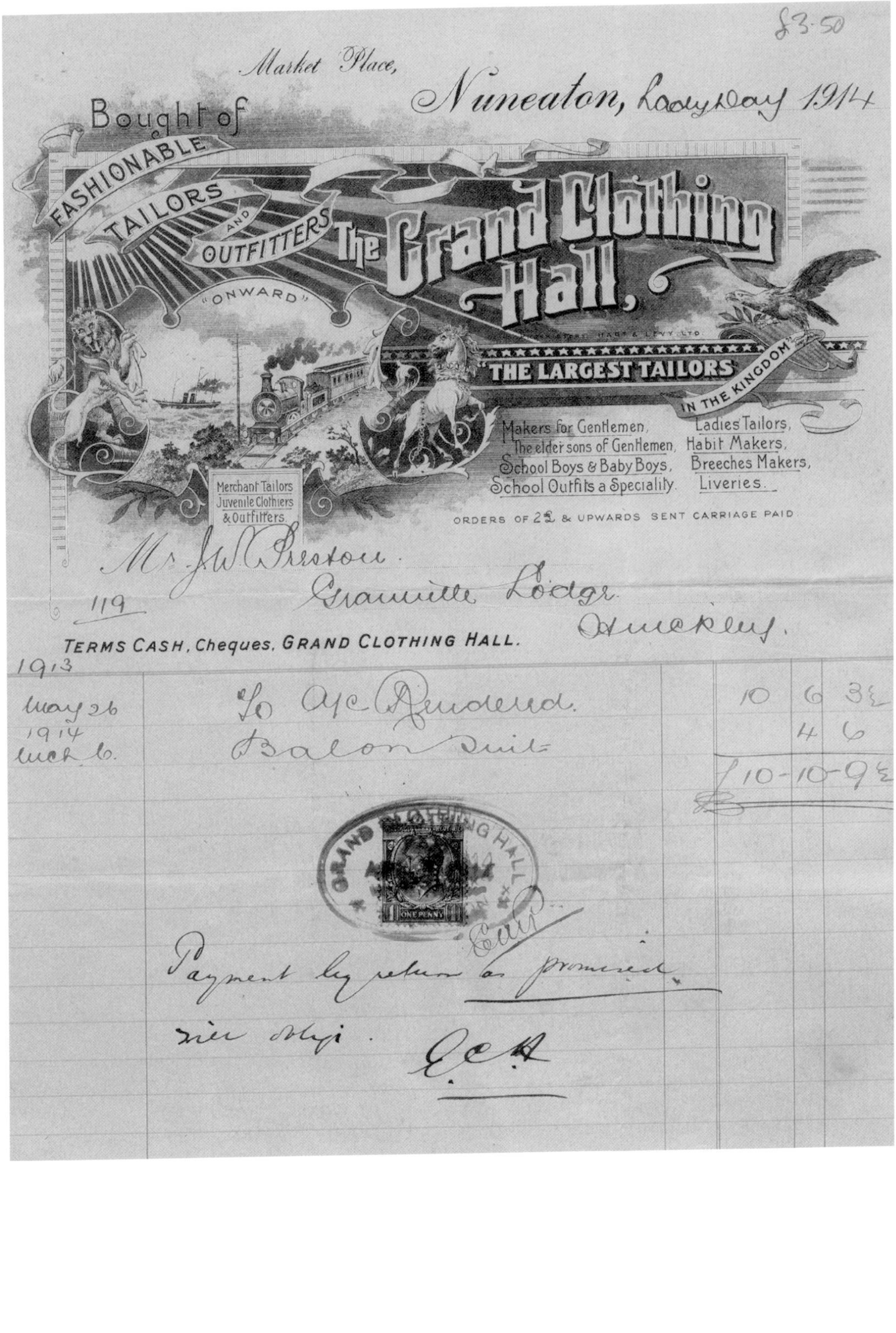

£3·50

Market Place,

Bought of

Nuneaton, Lady Day 1914

FASHIONABLE TAILORS AND OUTFITTERS
"ONWARD"

The Grand Clothing Hall,

THE LARGEST TAILORS IN THE KINGDOM

Makers for Gentlemen,
The elder sons of Gentlemen,
School Boys & Baby Boys,
School Outfits a Speciality.

Ladies Tailors,
Habit Makers,
Breeches Makers,
Liveries.

Merchant Tailors
Juvenile Clothiers
& Outfitters.

ORDERS OF 2£ & UPWARDS SENT CARRIAGE PAID

Mr J. W. Preston.
Granville Lodge,
Atherley.

119

TERMS CASH, Cheques, GRAND CLOTHING HALL.

1913					
May 26	To A/c Rendered.		10	6	3½
1914 mch. 6.	Balow Suit		4	6	
			£10	10	9½

Payment by return as promised.

very obly.

G.C.H.

The Market Place from the opposite direction looking towards Bridge Street.

The Charter Mayor was Joseph Fielding Johnson (1848–1917) who provided his own mayoral chain on 9 November 1907. Joseph Fielding Johnson was the managing director of the Nuneaton Wool & Leather Co. and a director of Stanley Brothers Ltd as well as the ironmongery company of Parsons & Sherwin & Co. He lived at Attleborough Hall.

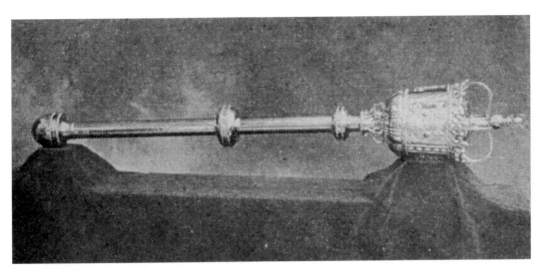

To celebrate its twenty-fifth anniversary a coat of arms was granted to the borough in 1932 and this insignia was inscribed on a mace which was given by the late Henry Lester in June that year.

COTON ROAD AND COUNCIL HOUSE, NUNEATON.   G.440.

In 1900 the land for the new town hall had been purchased from the proceeds of the sale of the old Market House. In 1931 the Birmingham firm of architects Messrs Peacock & Bewlay were commissioned by the borough council to build a new council house. Effectively the town had been without proper council offices since the sale of the Market House in 1899. Some offices had been used in the former fire station in Queen's Road but these were inadequate from the start. Construction commenced on the new town hall in 1931. Whittall & Son of Birmingham undertook the contract for a sum of £70,000 and completed the job ready for opening on 23 December 1933.

The council house dressed for its fiftieth anniversary celebrations on 29 July 1957. (Geoff Edmands)

Opposite: Riversley Park was opened to coincide with the granting of the Charter of Incorporation of the borough of Nuneaton in 1907. It was created on land given by Edward Melly. Most of the land had been water meadow and liable to flooding. It was mostly unsuited for building and part had been used as a municipal rubbish dump. Nevertheless, its fine open character gave the people of Nuneaton a valuable hint of countryside right in the heart of town. It brought a green wedge into the centre and was named Riversley after Mr Melly's former home in Liverpool. The Mellys were a distinguished family in the Liverpool area and were of Swiss descent.

Opening Ceremony in 1907 for the new park.

The Entrance Gates, Riversley Park Nuneaton
F. R. Jones' 'Charter' Series. No. 79

The entrance gateway to the newly opened park. This narrow entrance was opened out when Coton Road was made into a dual carriageway. The narrow road alongside which went to the Riversley Park Clinic was also widened and the railings removed. (Author's collection)

At the same time as the park was opened, Nuneaton Museum & Art Gallery was built. This photograph was taken sometime after the First World War when two large guns were placed alongside the building to commemorate the fallen men from Nuneaton. The guns were removed for scrap during the Second World War to aid the war effort. (Author's collection)

A war memorial was erected in the park. (Author's collection)

Various views of the new park were taken shortly after it was opened and issued as picture postcards. It will be noted that the river takes a different course to that we see today, being wider. When built the flow of the river was poorly understood – flooding took place on a regular basis up until the 1930s so it was decided to straighten it out to prevent a build-up of water behind the town weir. The banks were also built-up for this reason and the river narrowed to the width we see today. (Author's collection)

Riversley Park, Nuneaton.

This postcard view shows the island which once stood in the middle of the river opposite the bandstand. The park had not been open for long. The newly planted trees and the buildings in the background are on Coton Road. (Author's collection)

Riversley Park, Nuneaton.

Boating on the river Anker in the park. The bridge carries the pathway from the park up to Attleborough Road at the back of what is now Sainsbury's but was then the Nuneaton Wool & Leather Co. The pathway is just visible in a gap in the trees on the right. You can see the Wool & Leather works' chimney in the background. (Author's collection)

Opening day, 6 July 1907, and crowds gather around the brand new bandstand where the opening speeches were made. (Author's collection)

Nuneaton volunteers' band enters the park through an entrance no longer open to the public from Attleborough Road. A house called Drachenfels, named after a house on the Rhine in Germany, is on the right. (F.R. Jones, Charter Series)

The park shortly after opening looking towards the town. The trees, newly planted then, have grown to maturity a century later. (Author's collection).

Below and opposite above: Various views of a wintry day in the park, 5 January 1971. (Geoff Edmands)

The snowy exit from the park towards Attleborough Road. Sainsbury's store is now on the left but in those days it was the Union Wool & Leather factory which backed onto this pathway. (Author's collection)

The pathway in the previous photograph came up to Attleborough Road. The gateway stone pillar is on the extreme left. We are looking towards Church Street with St Nicolas parish church on the right. The soft-grey Attleborough stone wall on the right was engraved with many initials and messages to sweethearts now long departed. Part of the wall was taken down to reduce its height. Blocks from the demolished section are scattered by the river Anker further along Attleborough Road. (Author's collection)

A similar view but nearer to town taken about the same time as the previous photograph. (Author's collection)

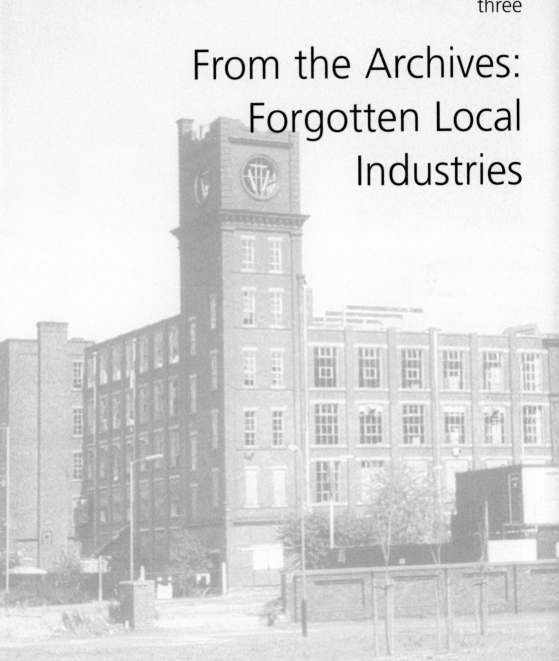

three

From the Archives: Forgotten Local Industries

A 1920s view of the mill. (Steve Casey collection)

Opposite above: Prior to nationalisation in 1947 three collieries in the Warwickshire area had laboratory facilities. Following on from this a laboratory for all the pits in the area was set up at Wilnecote. In 1958 the National Coal Board purchased Tansey's needle factory in Corporation Street, Nuneaton and this became fully operational as a laboratory on 27 July 1959. This is the laboratory as newly opened. (Courtesy Alan Croshaw)

Opposite below: Courtaulds was such a feature of town life with its distinctive clock. It was a huge building and employed many local people (1,050 in 1957), mostly girls, and when they married they had to leave for the company's employment – rules were strictly observed. Courtaulds Ltd was the largest rayon manufacturer in the British Commonwealth. They had twenty-four factories and employed 27,000 people. They also made nylon and cellophane. The rayon was used in textile manufacture for the home market and export and was also woven into fabric in the company's own textile mills. (Author's collection)

Above: A view from Marlborough Road. The same firm that built Big Ben, Gillett and Johnson of Croydon built Courtaulds clock. (Author's collection)

Courtaulds LIMITED
MARLBOROUGH RD., NUNEATON

Courtaulds Factory, Nuneaton.

The HOUSE FOR QUALITY
OF PRODUCTS & EMPLOYEES

Good employees require good working conditions, to which Courtaulds have given due consideration, amenities include:

Good canteen facilities : moderate prices : subsidised meals for juniors. Superbly equipped surgery: adequate medical services. Convalescent Home. Dental Service for juniors. Well-stocked Library. Efficient Works Council, consisting of employer and employee representatives. Apprentice Training Scheme. Up-to-date Works Magazine. Holidays with Pay. Grant to employees in Services. Excellent Sports Club at Higham Lane ; football ; hockey ; cricket ; tennis; bowls; billiards, etc.

Our products are, and will be, in great demand all over the world, so, if you are interested in joining our organisation, call at the Local Office of THE MINISTRY OF LABOUR AND NATIONAL SERVICE, mentioning the name of COURTAULDS, for further particulars.

Opposite below: In the 1990s the factory, which had been derelict for some years, was pulled down. The only remnant today is one doorway left in isolation in Marlborough Road. The contractor has started the sad process of carefully knocking it down without disruption to the neighbouring houses. (Author's collection)

A business which prospered in a growing town like Nuneaton was the ironmongery firm of Parsons & Sherwins. Here we see their management and staff outside their extensive workshops in Newdigate Street. I do not have the names of any of the men. They all have their various caps and hats on and show quite

clearly their status in the firm. All the men at the front with bowler hats were senior managers and directors. Parsons supplied everything from screws and nails, candles and tools to petroleum, cars and agricultural implements, even erecting steel framed sheds for farmers and local industrial firms. (Author's collection)

Nuneaton's Weaving of to-day (M

One of the oldest trades in Nuneaton was silk ribbon weaving. It had been the staple means of employment of Nuneaton up until the 1830s but a slump brought about much unemployment and poverty although a large proportion of the population still earned their living from it until about 1860 when the business almost died out. Factory production methods concentrated the remnants of the trade into a few small firms including Henry Slingsby & Sons. As ribbons in clothing died away new uses were found for silk products: regalia and medal ribbons of all kinds for military uniforms, civic and friendly society use, silk pictures, book marks, Masonic aprons, banners, scarves, clothes labels, collars and so on. Slingsby's products were shipped

all over the country and to the colonies. By 1909 it was one of the biggest silk producers in England. The business was originally started in 1848 by Henry Slingsby and was then carried on by his son Henry and his grandsons Montague and Guilford Slingsby. Henry retired in 1920. The work carried out was so fine that the shuttle in the loom moved backwards and forwards 700 times to 1in of ribbon. A Coventry manufacturer (Franklins) took over the business in the late 1940s when the Nuneaton factory closed. This photograph was taken in 1907 as part of the Charter Day celebrations. Slingsby's float was one of the many provided by local businesses that passed through the town representing the trades in the district. (Author's collection)

TUTTLE HILL GRANITE MACADAM
JUDKINS LIMITED

am Rock Drill and Samples of Macadam (Judkins, Ltd.)
F. R. JONES . . . . SERIES . No.

Two floats which took part in the borough celebrations of 1907 were the stone-quarrying firms of Judkins and William Griffiths. Judkins quarry was at Tuttle Hill and was a very old business which owned a stone quarry that had been in use for over 200 years. (Author's collection)

Opposite above: Haunchwood Brick & Tile Co. Ltd at Stockingford was one of the most successful brick makers in the Midlands. This view was taken over the stockyard on a snowy day, 9 January 1959. Modernisation was carried out in 1960, which involved a waste heat recovery scheme, introduction of electric-driven machinery in place of the old steam engines and rebuilding parts of the site for new equipment. Unfortunately, ten years later the brickyard was closed. (Geoff Edmands)

Opposite below: On 17 April 1971 Mr E.C. Richardson, a former senior manager with the company, revisited the old site as it is demolished. (Geoff Edmands)

William Griffith's quarry was at Griff. They had ninety-eight employees at one time. Their head office was in London. Although it says Griff Granite Quarries on the float, their main product was basalt. The quarry closed in the 1950s. (Author's collection)

four

Old Transport

Nowadays we think of the Nags Head in Queen's Road as an old building but it was, in effect, the third one to be seen in the town within living memory of old-timers when it was opened in 1927. The oldest one was this tiny pub, which used to be in Coventry Street and may have dated back to the 1700s. A more modern pub replaced it around 1900. The old Nags Head was a starting point for carters taking bulk quantities of silk ribbons to Coventry where they were sent onto London through middlemen. Nuneaton people only received a fraction of the selling price of the ribbon when it reached its destination in the shops and clothing manufactories of London. Many Nuneaton people lived around the Cripplegate and Wood Street area in the east end of London as they sometimes migrated there to help out in the silk warerooms, or in some cases their families had become wealthy, cutting out the middleman, and became silk manufacturers and merchants as well.

Right: Remember the old bath chair, the method of transport for disabled people before the days of the wheelchair? (Author's collection)

Below: A photograph of what must have been the predecessor of the method of transport we would term today a van delivery. A small cart pulled by a mule was used to transport light loads throughout the district. The photograph was taken in Nuneaton but we do not know who the deliveryman was, what he was carrying in his boxes or the date. (Author's collection)

Above: Flooding was common in Nuneaton. In this view of Dugdale Street in 1932 it presents no problems to the horse and cart but must have been a nuisance to those homes flooded this far away from the river. (Ian Hickman)

Opposite above: A row of old cottages pulled down in the 1960s. On the right is Collins cycle store. Three of these young people are known. From left to right: Beth Harris, -?-, Alan Beamish, Jack Harris. (Ian Hickman)

Opposite below: Nuneaton had at one time a steam-powered, horse-drawn fire pump named by the local crew 'The George Eliot'. The man sitting behind the big wheel to the right of the nameplate is George Green but who are the others in this view? The photograph is taken in the fire station yard off Queen's Road around 1900. The old steam fire engine finished up in McDonagh's scrapyard where it was broken up.

Above: Horse transport lingered on in Nuneaton up until recent times although it is very rare to see a gypsy caravan in town today. This view shows an authentic gypsy caravan in Coventry Road on 16 August 1959. (Geoff Edmands)

Left: A gypsy caravan on its way, at walking pace, by the Whitestone on a very slow journey to Wales, 1980. (Geoff Edmands)

Opposite below: At one time you could park in the Market Place. A selection of 1950s and 1960s models crowd for space on the only stretch of parking then available along a 70ft stretch of pavement. No fear of traffic wardens in those days. After this picture was taken in 1968 parking was banned in the Market Place. The gable ends of the Red Lion pub can be seen on the left. (*Coventry Evening Telegraph*)

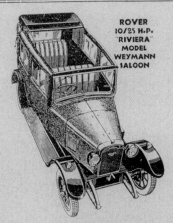

Above: Old cars and their retailers are often overlooked in local history. A principal garage in Nuneaton belonged to Sam Robbins Ltd. When he started selling bicycles from a shop in Abbey Street, and a car showroom built on the corner of Leicester Road and Bondgate, he had almost an entire monopoly of the motor trade in Nuneaton. The business was started about 1893 in Rugby and expanded to Nuneaton and Willenhall in Staffordshire. From the humblest beginnings the business expanded into carriage and furniture making, furniture removal and storage, jewellery and plates, organs, pianos and musical instruments, auctioneers, house agents and valuers.

Arthur Cooper Cars was a well-known car dealer in Princes Street. This photograph was taken on 3 October 1970. (Geoff Edmands)

A view of Newdigate Square where George Eliot's statue now stands. (*Coventry Evening Telegraph*)

The Market Place in the 1950s. Barclays Bank is on the left, and Coventry Street is off to the left of the picture.

In 1978 the narrow roadway of Abbey Gate was pedestrianised due to the danger posed by lorries which mounted the pavement as they tried to negotiate this tight little street. This caused a great deal of danger to pedestrians. The proposal, first mooted in 1973, took five years to implement at a cost of £8,000. (*Coventry Evening Telegraph*)

Now and then a car would come to grief, and a view taken in Coventry Road on 2 July 1961 shows a Standard soft top, which has hit a bus stop being rescued by a breakdown truck from Redgate Motors. (Geoff Edmands)

Mr Frank Tonks of Haunchwood Brick & Tile Co. Ltd stands by his 1955 Ford Zephyr on 24 August 1959. (Geoff Edmands)

Monty's had a motley collection of buses including this one parked up near their depot in Attleborough. (In the background is a fine cypress tree, which stood for many years in the grounds of Attleborough Hall.) MDE 333 was an AEC Regal III with Strachan body seating thirty-five, built in 1950 and bought secondhand from Silcox of Pembroke Dock in May 1959. It was sold in June 1963 but subsequent owners are not known. (Author's collection)

NUNEATON GAS COMPANY.

GAS is the IDEAL FUEL. NO LABOUR

Call at the Gas Works and ask for what you want and you will get it!

GAS Costs no more than Coal. NO DIRT OR ASHES!

Stop the driver of this Car, or call at the Gas Works and ask for particulars of our All Gas House Scheme.

GEORGE HELPS, Engineer & Manager, Gas Works, NUNEATON.

Nuneaton Gas Co. whose works was in Queen's Road had its own van. This advertisement probably dates back to the 1920s. In the background are the retorts in the gas works yard. The Nuneaton Gas Co. under the direction of George Helps was very innovative and Mr Helps perfected the technique of gasification of low quality coal, thereby reducing the cost of coal gas. (Author's collection)

Opposite above: A view of the Market Place end of Bridge Street in 1958 shows clearly the bottleneck that then existed for traffic along this street which led to its widening. This had been talked about from the 1920s but it is sad to say that this was soon deemed unnecessary after widening was completed as road traffic was banned from Bridge Street and pedestrianisation took place. The Lants lorry is delivering pop to the Bull Hotel. The British Road Services truck is a flatbed. Behind is a lorry belonging to K.V. Day & Sons of Glenfield, near Leicester. (Jenkins & Son)

Mishaps came in all forms on the road. In this 1974 view a low-loader has grounded itself on Coventry Road Canal Bridge by the Wharfe Inn. (Author's collection)

Another form of transport you do not see these days is the bicycle-propelled knife grinder. Here Mr Barrett has set up his treadle about to sharpen a knife on 9 September 1966. (Geoff Edmands)

On 20 May 1965 petrol, depending on grade, cost 5s 6d or 5s 3d per gallon. This is Carol Smith on the left and Inos Margitte at the Agip Service Station on Midland Road. Agip is no longer a brand known in Nuneaton but is still found in continental Europe. (Geoff Edmands)

Many Nuneaton people set off for Skegness (or Skeggy as it was affectionately known to holidaymakers throughout the Midlands), for their summer holidays. Here is a Lloyd's service to that east-coast holiday resort about to depart on 26 July 1959. (Geoff Edmands)

Nuneaton Corporation employed a large number of specialised vehicles over the years including this road sweeper. Seen here in Tompkinson Road in 1950, a workman is also sweeping the pavements. (Keith Draper collection)

Above: The Hippodrome picture house and theatre made a distinctive backdrop around 1960 for the bus parking area at the back of Nuneaton bus station. Here a No. 754 service is parked up for a while. (Author's collection)

Looking underneath the bridge carrying the Nuneaton–Coventry railway line over Attleborough Road in the 1960s. Just beyond the bridge immediately to the left can be seen the wall at the front of Fielding Johnsons mill. The Midland Red bus is on the 765 route which ran from Coventry–Nuneaton–Atherstone–Tamworth–Lichfield. *(Coventry Evening Telegraph)*

Opposite below: The Coventry Canal is a corridor through Nuneaton that has stood the test of time. Here we can see the stretch between Griff and Chilvers Coton on an icy day in January 1959. At that time the length was also traversed by telephone poles. These have now been cut down. (Geoff Edmands)

Griff Hollows, 9 February 1969. The old road was being widened. The new road takes shape to the left of the old road. (Geoff Edmands)

Opposite above: An empty working narrow boat traveling along the Coventry Canal steered by an elderly boatwoman passes under the Boot Bridge at Coton on 17 September 1967. (Geoff Edmands)

Opposite below: Two working narrow boats turning in the wide section at the old limekilns at the bottom of Tuttle Hill on 17 September 1967. (Geoff Edmands)

If you drive north-west on Watling Street you will see rising up on your left the Nuneaton ridge. This has been extensively quarried over the years and none more so than in the Hartshill area. This photograph taken in the 1960s shows the conical tip of Jees. Views from the top of the Nuneaton ridge afford great panoramas across the whole of Leicestershire away to the Charnwood Forest. (Keith Draper collection)

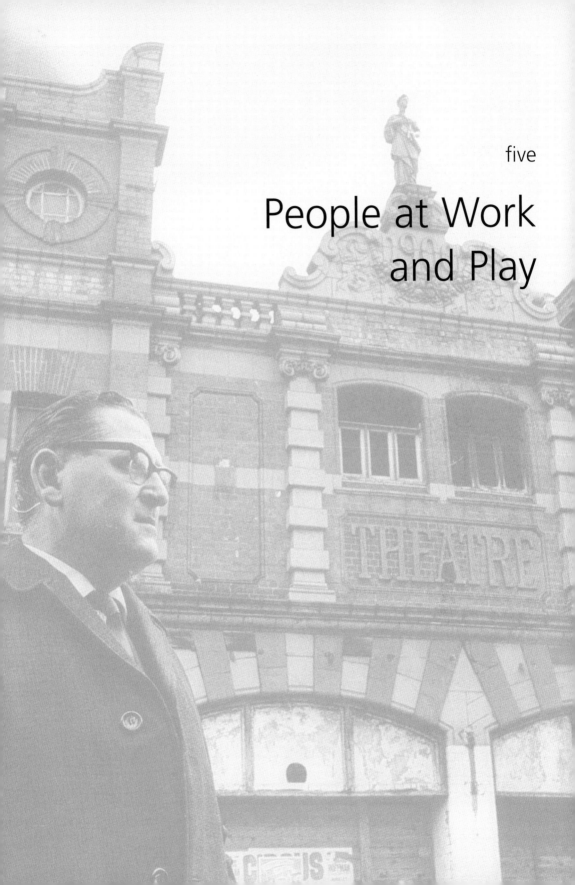

five

People at Work
and Play

Attleborough Church School included gardening in their curriculum. These boys look proud of their activities. The year is 1925. (*Midlands County Tribune & Warwickshire County Graphic*)

Opposite above: Ruby Sargeant at the switchboard at Lindley Lodge, the National Coal Board headquarters on Watling Street near Nuneaton, on 17 September 1960. (Geoff Edmands)

Opposite below: An unknown group of competitors display their prize marrows, turnips, beetroot and other fine vegetables for the Reader Challenge Cup at Tuttle Hill Allotments during 1914-1915. (Author's collection)

Above: Mrs Bell's concert party in 1925 at Fitton Street Evening School gave their activities free of charge to a number of charitable institutions. Back row: Miss E. Wayne, Miss N. Diskin, Miss O. Wayne. Middle: Miss Nixon, Miss A. Whitehead, Miss L. Crolla, Miss Kiteley, Miss M. Fowler. Front: Miss L. Merry, Mrs Ford. (*Midlands County Tribune & Warwickshire County Graphic*)

Left: Mr Walter Coles was manager of the Midland Bank and a popular local amateur entertainer. (*Midlands County Tribune & Warwickshire County Graphic, 1925*)

Nuneaton Queen's Road girls' netball team, winners of the Alderman French Shield in 1925. Back row: E. Farmer, F. Kenning, P. Frettsome, D. Camm. Sitting: Margaret Thompson, May Thompson and D. Grayley. (*Midlands County Tribune & Warwickshire County Graphic*)

Mr A.K. Knox, managing director of Haunchwood Brick & Tile Co. Ltd, presents a clock and medal for fifty years' service to Mr H. Jephcote (foreman) in the company's offices on 24 January 1964. Next to Mr Jephcote are Doug Bosley, Dennis Portman, Joe Tonks, Pat Sherriff, A.L. Norton (sales manager) E.W. Daffern, Jacqueline Rogers, Mr H.C. Rogers (works manager), E.C. Richardson, H. Burdett, and Geoff Edmands. (Geoff Edmands)

Opposite above: Mr T.R. Barratt of Nuneaton, winner of the 100 yards club handicap race, with the four cups he has held since 1921 at a swimming gala in Nuneaton in July 1925. (*Midlands County Tribune & Warwickshire County Graphic*)

Opposite below: A lesson in anatomy for the Griff Colliery Division St John Ambulance. Top row: Cpl Pettit, Cpl Stow, Privates Smith, Harper, Baker, Owen, Lamprey, Harvey, Lyons, T. Lees, Daley, Dickens, Marlow, Chandler and Wright. Middle: Supt Ashby Randle, Povey Harper, T. Wallen, George Neath, Cpl G. Brain. Front: Privates W. Smith and Bazeley. (*Midlands County Tribune & Warwickshire County Graphic*)

Above and below: In 1967 whilst site works were being carried out for a new building merchant's yard, Groves, Harper & Co., a medieval pottery kiln was uncovered and a band of intrepid archaeologists carried out a very thorough dig to record the find before it was concreted over. (Geoff Edmands)

Above: The former Hippodrome cinema and theatre stood derelict for some years after closure. It is pictured here in July 1968. It was regarded as an eyesore and pulled down, its happy days forgotten. The statue was saved by the demolition company and now happily resides in Nuneaton Museum. (*Coventry Evening Telegraph*)

Right: In March 1948 this pretty girl, Mary Lucas, appeared as Susan in the *Desert Song*, which was produced by the Nuneaton Amateur Dramatic Society and staged at the Hippodrome Theatre. (Author's collection)

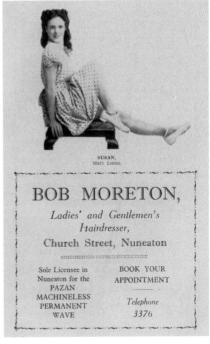

SUSAN,
Mary Lucas.

These two pages and next one: Members of Nuneaton Town Council in 1925:

Cllr F. Marriott, Stockingford Ward.

Cllr G. Taylor, chairman of the Highways Committee, representative of St Mary's Ward.

Cllr D. King representative of Stockingford Ward.

Cllr A. Roberts, St Nicholas Ward.

Cllr T. Daffern, representative of St Mary's Ward.

Cllr Joseph Bates, representative of Chilvers Coton Ward.

Alderman J.H.Cartwright

Cllr G. Harvey, St Nicholas Ward.

Alderman T. Horton J.P., a former mayor of
Nuneaton.

Cllr Dr L.E.Price, representative of Chilvers
Coton Ward.

Alderman T. W. Sands J.P., a former mayor of
Nuneaton.

Alderman J. Randle J.P., a former mayor of
Nuneaton.

Right: Alfred Lester Scrivener (1845–1886), founding editor of the *Nuneaton Observer*, was Nuneaton and district's greatest local historian. He founded the *Nuneaton Observer* with his partner William Wilson in 1877. Later he moved to Bootle near Liverpool in 1881 where he became editor of the *Bootle Times*. (Pat Roberts)

Below: At the beginning of the twentieth century it was possible to reel in a lot of fish in the river Anker. Here is local sportsman and expert angler – 'Sixer' Moreton (in the middle) with friends posing with their splendid catch. (John Burton Collection)

George W. Clare Speight took a studio picture of Freda Halford with her dog in his studio in Coton Road Nuneaton. Clare Speight was a brilliant photographer whose superb quality photographs are much sought after today. He was born in Rugby the son of Edward Hall Speight who was first listed as a photographer at Long Lawford in 1872. Edward Speight was the official photographer to Rugby School. The family continued in business as photographers until the 1930s whilst Clare moved to Nuneaton about 1890 and opened a studio there. In 1892 he produced a set of postcards depicting Nuneaton scenes. (Anne Paling Lawson)

This pretty Nuneaton girl was Margaret Muscutt (1906–1924). She died very young, aged eighteen. (Anne Paling Lawson)

Other local titles published by Tempus

Memories of Atherstone
CHRISTINE FREEMAN

This book brings together the personal memories of people who have lived and worked in Atherstone, vividly recalling childhood and schooldays, shops and working life, leisure and entertainment and the war years. It is the people, whose experiences and reminiscences are recorded here, who have shaped the area into the fascinating place it is today. The many absorbing stories are complemented by over 100 photographs from the participants' private collections.

0 7524 3422 5

Haunted Coventry
DAVID MCGRORY

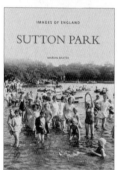

When Coventry sleeps, the dead wander the streets! Or so it is said in *Haunted Coventry*, which features spooky stories from the city and surrounding area. Within these pages you will find the Phantom Monk of St Mary's Hall, ghostly grey ladies, a spectre which appears to do the washing up and the Devil himself, rattling chains at Whitefriars. From spectres in the suburbs to haunted pubs, this fascinating collection of strange sightings and happenings in the city is sure to appeal to anyone intrigued by Coventry's haunted heritage.

0 7524 3708 9

Sutton Park
MARIAN BAXTER

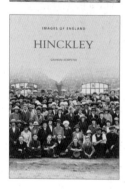

The largest local authority park of its type in England, Sutton Park is the remnant of an extensive forest that once covered much of the Midlands and has retained many ancient features. The park's diverse landscape encompasses woodland, heathland, wetlands and marshes, as well as seven pools which attract a wide variety of wildlife rarely seen in this region. With over 170 archive photographs, this book looks at the history and heritage of this jewel in the crown of Birmingham.

0 7524 4069 1

Hinckley
GRAHAM KEMPSTER

The lives and times of Hinckley over more than a century are illustrated in this fascinating collection of old photographs, selected from the archives of the *Hinckley Times*. The Hinckley Carnival is represented plus some of the many local football teams that existed before the war. Prepare to be surprised by a picture showing the huge number of people that turned out to see the new bandstand opened in the park in 1908!

0 7524 3619 8

If you are interested in purchasing other books published by Tempus, or in case you have difficulty finding any Tempus books in your local bookshop, you can also place orders directly through our website

www.tempus-publishing.com